The Messianic Claims

Of

Gail A. Riplinger

"All for the Greater Glory of Gail"

Pastor Phil Stringer, Ph.D.

ISBN 978-1-56848-100-5

Published by:
The Dean Burgon Society
Box 354, Collingswood, New Jersey 08108
www.DeanBurgonSociety.org
October, 2010

BIBLE FOR TODAY NUMBER: #3479
Web: www.biblefortoday.org
E-mail: bft@biblefortoday.org

Bible For Today, Inc.
900 Park Ave.
Collingswood, New Jersey 08108

Formatted by The Old Paths Publications
H. D. & Patricia Williams, Directors
142 Gold Flume Way
Cleveland, GA 30528

Web: www.TheOldPathsPublications.com
E-mail: TOP@theoldpathspublications.com

1.0

DEDICATION

This work is dedicated to all who love the Truth.

*Sanctify them through thy **truth**: thy word is **truth**.*

John 17:17

*Jesus saith unto him, I am the way, the **truth**, and the life: no man cometh unto the Father, but by me.*

John 14:6

*Howbeit when he, the Spirit of **truth**, is come, he will guide you into all truth: for he shall not speak of himself; but whatsoever he shall hear, that shall he speak: and he will shew you things to come.*

John 16:13

*But the hour cometh, and now is, when the true worshippers shall worship the Father in spirit and in **truth**: for the Father seeketh such to worship him.*

John 4:23

*And ye shall know the **truth**, and the **truth** shall make you free.*

John 8:32

3

"Lastly, how was it to have been believed that the Revisionists would show themselves industrious in sowing broadcast over four continents doubts as to the **Truth** of Scripture, which it will never be in their power either to remove or to recal?" [Dean John William Burgon, Revision Revised, Article II, 1883, Reprinted by the Dean Burgon Society, September, 2000, p. 115 (p. 160 in the PDF Version)]

TABLE OF CONTENTS

PREFACE

The Importance of the King James Bible

Next year, 2011, marks the 400th anniversary of the Authorized King James Bible. No book on earth has been more responsible for shaping Western Civilization. This book is the foundation upon which America was built. The fundamentalist movement was born believing, defending, and using the KJB. Even as textual criticism gained a foothold in many of our fundamentalist colleges and universities, the KJB continued to reign in our pulpits. For many of us the KJB will always remain God's final English Bible standard until Christ returns. A spiritual revival through a return to faith in and preaching of the KJB remains the last best hope of our nation, our churches, our families, and our faith.

Confusion Over the King James Bible

Our independent Baptist churches are divided and confused as never before over the Accuracy and Authority of the King James Bible. 1 Corinthians 14:33 says:

> *"For God is not the author of confusion, but of peace, as in all churches of the saints."*

God has blessed Dr. Phil Stringer with the skill to help explain one growing aspect of this division created between two extreme camps that are defending the KJB. One camp stresses using only the God's original Hebrew, Aramaic and Greek text as their source for Bible translation. The other camp stresses using only the KJB for all Bible translation work. They hold the KJB as superior to all other Bible versions including God's inspired Hebrew, Aramaic, and Greek words underlying the foundation of the KJB.

There Is No Need to Correct The KJB

Dr. Stringer and I have many good friends on both sides of this issue. We have no desire to offend or weaken the faith of anyone on either side who continues to believe, use, and defend the KJB. We reject all "so-called correction" of the KJB by any other source or language including the Hebrew, Aramaic, and Greek. We do not believe it is humanly possible to make changes in the KJB to improve upon either the accuracy and/or authority of the words in the KJB. We accept by faith the KJB as God's final appointed English Bible standard given to us by God's divine providential preservation. I concur with Dr. Stringer's statement:

> "For the record's sake, I believe that the King James Bible is pure, perfect, infallible and inerrant. For 399 years it has impacted the world for Christ in a way that no other translation ever has. There is nothing in it that needs to be replaced or changed."

Divisions Must Be Pointed Out

It has been my policy and practice not to publicly attack any believer who uses and defends the King James Bible. Yet the Bible says in Romans 16:17:

> "Now I beseech you, brethren, mark them which

cause divisions and offences contrary to the doctrine which ye have learned; and avoid them."

I believe Dr. Stringer has proven there are some important doctrinal matters confronting us. Therefore I am penning this preface in obedience to God's Holy Scripture. I gave a very favorable report on Gail Riplinger's book, *New Age Bible Versions,* in 1992 at the Dean Burgon Society Annual Meeting. I still believe Gail Riplinger is very intelligent and has done a lot of excellent research.

To the best of my knowledge, up until the present conflict, Gail Riplinger remained friends with Dr. and Mrs. Waite, Dr. DiVietro, Dr. Williams, Dr. Stringer and many of us in the Dean Burgon Society for many years. As in the past, I will continue to pray for her daily that God will work His will in her heart and life. She is a very talented person. It is my hope that Mrs. Riplinger will recognize her mistakes and reconcile herself to her estranged brothers and sisters in Christ whom she has erroneously criticized. I sincerely believe that this book, when read and properly assimilated, can have a positive part in that remedial process.

The Start & Primary Thrust of the Controversy

What really started this controversy? Someone reported publicly on Gail Riplinger's previous marriages and divorces. The Waites heard about this and approached her and they said she denied the truth of the report. The Waites still believed her and defended her cover up until they discovered the truth in legal documents. While this was the apparent start of the controversy, it is not the primary thrust of Dr. Stringer's book. I can concur with Dr. Stringer's past thinking and words:

> "As recently as March, 2009, I said from the pulpit of the church I pastor, 'Gail Riplinger is a gracious Christian lady who has devoted herself to defending the King James Bible. I simply must disagree with her about a few things. I would not say anything similar today.'"

An Apology

He has provided many facts in this book about Gail Riplinger of which I and many others had remained ignorant and unaware. So, as a supporter of Gail Riplinger's work in the beginning, I owe all my brethren in the DBS an apology for not being more alert and aware of the changes as they became evident in Gail Riplinger's life and work. I thank Dr. Stringer for having the courage, and taking the time to discover and put in print a number of facts many of us did not know. Thank you!, Dr. Stringer, for giving me the privilege of writing this preface to your work.

The Traditional Foundation of the KJB

To defend the KJB as superior to the inerrant, infallible Hebrew, Aramaic, and Greek words God first revealed and recorded by verbal, plenary, inspiration is to discredit the historical and traditional foundation upon which the KJB rests. It is to deny the continuity of the inspired, inerrant, infallible body of truth God has preserved in Bibles for every generation of believers for thousands of years. God has not failed to keep his promises to preserve His truth pure in every generation. There is no new inspired truth in the KJB than that which God first gave by inspiration in the Hebrew, Aramaic, and Greek words which the KJB accurately translates. The KJB is pure, perfect, infallible and inerrant because the body of truth accurately translated into the KJB remains God's same body of inspired truth He has preserved from the beginning. That inspired truth has from eternity past been recorded in Heaven.

> *"For ever, O LORD, thy word is settled in heaven." (Psalm 119:89). "Known unto God are all his works from the beginning of the world." (Acts 15:18).*

God's Promises

Please read again prayerfully some of God's Promises to His people:

> *"As for me, this is my covenant with them, saith the LORD; My spirit that is upon thee, and my words which I have put in thy mouth, shall not depart out of thy mouth, nor out of the mouth of thy seed, nor out of the mouth of thy seed's seed, saith the LORD, from henceforth and for ever." (Isaiah 59:21). "The words of the LORD are pure words: as silver tried in a furnace of earth, purified seven times. ⁷Thou shalt keep them, O LORD, thou shalt preserve them from this generation for ever." (Psalm 12:6, 7).*

God has preserved his Words pure for thousands of years, even before there was an English language or a King James Bible.

My Beliefs Have Not Changed

Thirty years ago in my introduction to textual criticism entitled, *The Word of God on Trial*, I wrote in the Annotated

Bibliography the following words describing Dr. Waite and the Dean Burgon Society:

> Dr. Waite is president of the newly formed "Dean Burgon Society". He is doing some scholarly work in defense of the traditional Greek text and the King James Version of the Bible. He is also going on the offense against scholars who publicly attack our position. He recently published a book on the heresies of Westcott and Hort. He writes regular columns in "The Dean Burgon News," a monthly paper circulated by the society. The address of "The Dean Burgon Society" is Box 359, Collingswood, NJ 08108. The Dean Burgon Society is named after John William Burgon, the Dean of Chichester and greatest scholar and defender of the traditional Greek text of the churches and the King James Translation in the last century. His arguments were so complete and conclusive that all the revisionists avoided Burgon like the plague. One hundred years later we still find his books unanswered by the 'Bible Changers'. Now, in the 20th century, it will be ironic to see God use the name of Dean Burgon to spearhead the drive to victory and a return to the traditional text of the churches."

I continue to hold this same view of Dr. Waite and my brethren in the Dean Burgon Society into the 21st century.

This preface is a defense of the same strong position members of the Dean Burgon Society have held while defending the KJB for over 30 years. Gail Riplinger was once a friend toward us for many years while knowing our position on the Bible. Now, Gail Riplinger has started publicly attacking the Dean Burgon Society's defense of traditional Bible texts including the Hebrew, Aramaic, and Greek text underlying the

KJB. May God use Dr. Stringer's insight into the Riplinger changes and charges to help tear down the growing wall between us as opposing camps striving to defend the same God appointed King James Bible. As the late Baptist missionary J. J. Ray titled his book defending the KJB back in 1955: *God Wrote Only One Bible.*

The Author of Confusion

Satan is the author of confusion. As KJB believers and defenders we are all God's faithful remnant defending, as the late Dr. David Otis Fuller used to say, *"The Bible God Uses and Satan Hates."* Will you pray for the Holy Spirit to give you wisdom to read Dr. Stringer's book with an open heart and mind? As pastors of local independent Baptist Churches, neither Dr. Stringer nor I have any motivation or spare time to engage in unnecessary conflicts between brethren. We are motivated by a love for the truth of and defense of the faith *"once delivered"* to the saints and divinely preserved for us in the Authorized King James Bible.

> *"Beloved, when I gave all diligence to write unto you of the common salvation, it was needful for me to write unto you, and exhort you that ye should earnestly contend for the faith which was once delivered unto the saints." (Jude 1:3).*

Defending our faith in the KJB is not a choice! We must contend for the faith!

Dr. Robert J. Barnett, Pastor
Calvary Baptist Church
Grayling , Michigan 49738

13

*For thy lovingkindness is before mine eyes: and I have walked in thy **truth**.*

Psalms 26:3

The Messianic Claims
of
Gail Riplinger

"All for the Greater Glory of Gail"

by Dr. Phil Stringer

"The simple believeth every word; but the prudent looketh well to his going." Proverbs 14:15

Messiah—"any long awaited liberator." (*Webster Illustrated Contemporary Dictionary*, def. 3.)

Megalomania—"a mental disorder in which the subject thinks himself great or exalted." (Webster Illustrated Contemporary Dictionary.)

It is a shame that this monograph needs to be written. However, the circumstances demand it!

*LORD, who shall abide in thy tabernacle? who shall dwell in thy holy hill? He that walketh uprightly, and worketh righteousness, and speaketh the **truth** in his heart.*

Psalms 15:1-2

CHAPTER 1
THE GREAT DEBATE

The Two Positions

A tremendous debate rages among independent Baptist circles over Bible translation. This influences mission boards, Bible colleges, and printing ministries.

On the extremes of this debate are two positions concerning the source texts for Bible translation. One extreme is the "Greek and Hebrew only" group. They believe that all Bible translation must be done directly from the Greek and Hebrew languages.

Another extreme is the "English only" group. They believe that all Bible translation must be done directly from the King James Bible.

This tension is seen in the reaction to the revision of the Spanish Bible headed up by Humberto Gomez. He used three source texts: the 1602 Reina Valera Bible, the Greek and Hebrew Traditional Texts, and the King James Bible. These were all diligently compared and studied in an effort to provide the most accurate possible Spanish Bible.

The "Greek and Hebrew only" crowd have viciously attacked Humberto. Calvin George and some (but not all) of the leadership of the Trinitarian Bible Society have vilified Dr. Gomez for using the King James Bible as a source text. However, Gail Riplinger and most (but not all) of her supporters have attacked him aggressively because the King James Bible was not his only source text.

This same scenario is taking place in many languages around the world.

Genuine Bible translators should be able to relate to a

section of the famous poem, "The Charge of the Light Brigade":
> "Cannons to the right of them,
> Cannons to the left of them,
> Cannons in front of them"

Who Is Pushing This Debate

No one is pushing this debate with greater fervor than author and Bible teacher, Gail Riplinger.

Both the King James translators and those that worked with William Carey used multiple source texts. The King James Bible is the most successful Bible translation in the history of the world. Perhaps we could learn something from their work.

The King James Bible translators used: (as quoted by Gail Riplinger in *Hazardous Materials*, p. 1019),

> "the originall sacred tongues, together with comparing of the labours both of our own [previous English Bibles] and other foreign languages [Chaldee, Syriac, Spanish, French, Italian, Dutch] of many men who went before us..."

There is a better way to do Bible translation—than either "Greek only" or "English only." Use as many good source texts as possible.

Something To Be Learned From William Carey

Perhaps something could be learned from the ministry of William Carey.

Carey was a shoemaker, Baptist pastor, Bible translator, and educator.

Carey was born in 1761 and baptized in 1783. He went to India as a missionary in 1793. He served 41 years without a furlough. He died and was buried in India in 1834.

Carey studied at least one chapter of the Bible every day in each of six languages: English, Koine Greek, Latin, French, German and Italian.

He has been called the Bengali Luther, the Wycliffe of the East, the Tyndale of our Time, the Polyglot of India, and a Plodder for Christ. He is commonly known as the Father of Modern Missions. He has been called the greatest linguist who ever lived.

He served as a Professor of Oriental Languages at a secular university (Fort William College, which became Calcutta University). He also started a Bible college, a medical hospital, a leper hospital, and a Christian liberal arts university, which accepted non-Christian students.

His mission teams translated the Bible into forty languages and dialects—seven complete Bibles and thirty-three New Testaments. They also produced eight grammars and three dictionaries. Carey produced four translations himself (Bengali, Hindi, Marathi and Sanskrit). He worked with other missionaries on translations and he supervised other translation efforts. In all of these efforts, the advice and aid of nationals was incorporated.

Carey's translation teams used any and all good sources available and usable by the translators. Greek and Hebrew were used when possible. The King James Bible was always present. Earlier Indian translations were used in producing later Indian translations.

Carey certainly accomplished more than any of the loud voices in the current debate.

Maybe we should be learning something from both the King James translators and William Carey.

Absurdities On Both Sides of the Debate

Absurdities have arisen on both sides. In a June 2006 internet exchange, Calvin George castigated Mickey Carter, and J. J. Ray and others for suggesting that hundreds of translations have been done from the King James Bible. He and his correspondents mocked Dr. Carter and the others for being uneducated and ignorant. One of the participants called King James Bible believers "retards."

Calvin George asserted that only four or five translations had been done from the King James Bible.

In reality the original statement that the King James Bible has been translated into hundreds of languages comes not from Dr. Carter or J. J. Ray, but from Winston Churchill (*History of the English Speaking Peoples*, one volume, Commager edition, p. 160).

> "It won an immediate and lasting triumph. Copies could be bought for as little as five shillings, and even with the inflated prices of today can still be purchased for this sum. It superseded all other versions. No new revision was deemed necessary for nearly three hundred years. In the crowded emigrant ships which sailed to the New World of America, there was little room for baggage. If the adventurers took books with them they took the Bible, Shakespeare, and later *Pilgrim's Progress*, and the Bible they mostly took with them was the Authorised Version of King James I. About ninety million complete copies are thought to have been published in the English language alone. It has been translated into more than 760 tongues. The Authorised Version is still the most popular in England and the United States. This may be deemed James' greatest achievement, for the impulse was largely his. The Scottish pedant built better than he knew. The scholars who produced this masterpiece are

mostly unknown and unremembered. But they
forged an enduring link, literary and religious,
between the English-speaking peoples of the
world."

I wish I knew where Churchill got his information! I wish I
had a list of the translations he referred to. One thing that I am
sure of—he is no "King James retard."

The "English only side" can also be absurd. One
Riplingerite preacher recently preached that we don't need to
know Greek and Hebrew because you can't order pizza in Koine
Greek or Masoretic Hebrew.

I consider myself an expert on ordering pizza. I have been
doing it weekly for decades. However, I must confess that there
are more important issues in Bible study than pizza.

Unfortunately, Gail Riplinger has become a major figure in
this debate. More than any other person, her personal claims
about herself figure into the nature of this debate.

*For the word of the LORD is right; and all his works are done in **truth**.*

Psalms 33:4

CHAPTER 2
MEGALOMANIA ON STEROIDS

Riplinger's Claims About Study Tools

Listen to the claims that Gail Riplinger makes about herself:

> "The reader is in for many surprises, some that will verge on riveting shock. Before *this* book, no one had ever critically examined the authors of Greek and Hebrew study tools." (*Hazardous Materials*, p. 13)

That's right! No one ever understood before Gail Riplinger. Without her, you would be forever ignorant.

> "The worse mistake a reader could make would be to suppose that, because an author is not mentioned in this book, his Greek or Hebrew study tools are safe. <u>All tools have been examined and ALL are corrupt</u>." (*Hazardous Materials*, p.37).

That's right! Gail Riplinger has studied everything. She has not missed anything.

> "That with which the reader may not agree or which the reader may not understand will be rectified upon reading *the entire* book. <u>All questions have been anticipated and are explained somewhere and in detail. Assuming, 'the author does not know or understand 'something' will only be possible if the entire book is not read</u>." (*Hazardous Materials*, p. 40).

That's right. Dr. Riplinger has anticipated all your questions. She has answered them all. It is not possible that the author misunderstands anything.

"Come feast with me at Jesus' feet. Discover how the Holy Bible may be studied and its words understood. . . This is the first book to unveil treasures in the Word of God, using tools from the new field of computational linguistics." (*In Awe of Thy Word*, p. 6).

All For The Greater Glory of Gail

That's right, no one knew these truths before Gail Riplinger. If you read her books, you are feasting at Jesus' feet.

"This book is the first and only history of the Holy Bible based on a word-for-word and letter-by-letter collection of ancient and early Bibles." (*In Awe of Thy Word*, p. 7).

That's right! No one understood the Bible before Gail Riplinger. First and only!

When has anyone, male, or female, ever made such claims about their work? All for the "Greater Glory of Gail!"

CHAPTER 3
TRUST DR. RIPLINGER TO TELL YOU WHAT THE GREEK MEANS!

Riplinger's Proclamation

"I have done all of the Greek work for the reader."
(*Hazardous Materials*, p. 42).

What a statement! Don't do any research. Don't check out anything for yourself. Gail Riplinger will tell you what the Greek means. Trust her as your authority. What kind of a Baptist allows someone do all of their thinking for them?

Riplinger Does Not Know Greek

This proclamation is all the stranger when you realize that Gail Riplinger does not know Greek.

In a May, 1994 radio interview with Dr. Wayne House, Dr. Riplinger was forced to admit that she cannot read Greek or Hebrew. While she does not explicitly state in her books that she knows Greek or Hebrew, she makes many statements that would make you think she is a Greek or Hebrew scholar.

Just suspend your conscious mind. Gail Riplinger will tell you what to think.

An Example

Dr. Riplinger's claims are reminiscent of those of Charles Taze Russell, founder of the Jehovah's Witnesses. He also presented himself as the sole "interpreter" of the Greek. When he was exposed by Baptist pastor J. J. Ross, Russell sued Pastor

Ross for slander. The following exchange took place during the trial:

> *Question:*   (Attorney Staunton)—"Do you know the Greek alphabet?"
> *Answer*:   (Russell)—"Oh yes."
> Question: (Staunton)—"Can you tell me the correct letters if you see them?"
> *Answer:*   (Russell)—"Some of them, I might make a mistake on some of them."
> Question: (Staunton)—"Would you tell me the names of those on top of the page, page 447 I have got here?"
> *Answer:*   (Russell)—"Well, I don't know that I would be able to."
> Question: (Staunton)—"You can't tell what those letters are, look at   them and see if you know?"
> *Answer:*   (Russell)—"My way...(he was interrupted at this point and not allowed to explain)
> Question: (Staunton)—"Are you familiar with the Greek language?"
> Answer: (Russell)—"No."
> (Walter Martin, *Kingdom of the Cults*, p. 43-4.)

Pastor Ross was found not guilty of slander.

You can be sure that if Dr. Riplinger had any legitimate credentials in Greek and Hebrew, she would be loudly trumpeting them.

Anyone can claim to know Greek and Hebrew and demand that you trust them to tell you what the Greek and Hebrew means. No wise person will believe them.

The New Messiah

Gail Riplinger presents herself as a "new messiah" come to set Baptists free from the influence of Greek and Hebrew. All for the "Greater Glory of Gail."

Will you let someone do all of your thinking for you? What megalomania it takes to offer yourself as the one to do the thinking for everyone!

What else must be the result of all this but general uncertainty, confusion, distress 1 A hazy mistrust of all Scripture has been insinuated into the hearts and minds of countless millions, who in this way have been forced to become doubters,- yes, doubters in the **Truth** of Revelation itself. One recals sorrowfully the terrible woe denounced by the Author of Scripture on those who minister occasions of falling to others :-' It must needs be that offences come; but woe to that man by whom the offence cometh! [Dean John William Burgon, Revision Revised, Article III, 1883, Reprinted by the Dean Burgon Society, September, 2000, p. 237 (p. 283 in the PDF).

CHAPTER 4
IS GAIL RIPLINGER REALLY
GOD'S SECRETARY?

Riplinger's Claim

In the January-February 1994 edition of the *"End Times Victorious Living Prophecy Newsletter,"* Gail Riplinger stated:

> "Daily, during the six years needed for this investigation, the Lord miraculously brought the needed materials and resources—much like the ravens fed Elijah. Each discovery was not the result of effort on my part, <u>but of the direct hand of God</u>—so much so that I hesitated to even put my name on the book. Consequently, I used G. A. Riplinger—God as author <u>and Riplinger as secretary</u>."

That is an incredible statement in Baptist circles. It is literally a claim to divine inspiration.

She further expands on this claim. In *"Testimony, Question and Answer"* (tape of an interview), she explains her role as God's secretary:

> "I used to look out the window at the little old ladies and think, *Oh, if I could rake the leaves or if I could just get out of bed.* But what God did over that period of six years—and I, and I said to the Lord, I said, "Lord, you know I quit my job to, to do this research for you. Why would you put me in such an incapacitated state where I can't do research?" And the Lord showed me over a period of years, that it wasn't gonna be me and research and library, <u>it was gonna be the Holy</u>

<u>Spirit showing me things, and He was gonna take me aside, just like He did Ezekiel</u>—Ezekiel was on one side for a year and on another side for a while, and he was dumb, and everything else. And the Holy Spirit was gonna do the work and this was gonna be His book, and it wasn't gonna be my book at some head, cognitive research-type thing. It was gonna be something that He was gonna do. . .And, essentially, what would happen I would lay in bed all day—not through laziness—I was, I couldn't move, I couldn't—I was in so much pain, it was just, ah, it's on the 50 on the Richter Scale with pain. And, so, ah, I'd lay in bed all day and I'd be in so much pain.

Well, when you lay in bed all day you can't sleep at night. And, so, He would, He would say to me at about ten o'clock at night, He'd say (laughs), He'd say, "Well, get up and work on the book," (laughs) and I'd say, "no, I'm too sick (laughs)." And He'd say, "Get up and work on the book," and I'd say, "No."—You see, we fought for 15 minutes every night for six years (laughs) and, ah, then after I told Him I was too sick, He'd say, "you're in too much pain to sleep, aren't you?" and I said, "Yeah, I know," and, so, He said, "Well, get up and work on the book." And, so I would always say, "I'm a woman and I don't think women should do this." (laughs) and He goes, "Get up and work on the book!" And, so, He goes, "<u>Women make fine secretaries—that's all we need here </u>(laughs)." So, um—but every night for six years we had this little fifteen-minute battle and I'd get up and I'd work on it, and I would sit there in that chair, for six years. And I don't know if you've ever been on a rollercoaster but you know how white your knuckles are when you're holding on for dear life, you know, because you think you're gonna fall out. Well, I was in so much pain that I would hold on with one hand to the chair—white knuckles—and in the other hand I'm writing this book. And I'd sit there for the first—next—ten minutes and finally, I said, "This is ridiculous, this is ridiculous (laughs)." I'd say, "Okay, Lord," you know. <u>And then the devil whispered in my ear and he would tell me, "If you quit working on that book, if you throw away what you've found, I'll leave you alone and you won't be in any pain." And I said, "Get thee behind me, Satan.</u> We're going forward with this thing." You know. I said, "In the, ah, Inquisition, people put up with this kind of stuff," and I said, "I can put up with it (laughs) too." . .And, so, for a period of six years, I worked on the book for about six to eight hours a day, researching, collating."

As of July 26, 2010, this recorded interview was still being sold on Gail Riplinger's website.

Riplinger's Conversation With God & Satan

This is a very amazing story with very specific claims. She claims that God inspired her just like He did Ezekiel. She claims that she was just a secretary—the words were the Holy Spirit's. She claimed a nightly conversation with God for six years. She claims that <u>Satan made a specific offer to heal her if she would stop serving as God's secretary</u>.

No wonder that Gail Riplinger often compares herself to the prophetess Deborah.

In 1993, Gail Riplinger debated James White on radio station KRAS. He challenged her on her bizarre "acrostic algebra" (her own private form of numerology).

Her only defense was, "The Lord gave that to me one night." And then, "The Lord gave me that formula."

When you bring this up, Dr. Riplinger's followers either try to change the subject or claim that she didn't mean for her words to be taken literally. However, you can't ignore this. Her entire "ministry" is based upon her claim to be "God's Secretary."

Do you believe that Gail Riplinger actually heard the voice of God every night for six years? Did she hear a voice? Did Satan directly speak to her? Was she inspired like Ezekiel?

Her claims are very specific! They are crucial to her "ministry."

If she really had these supernatural conversations—was it really God that she heard? Demons delight in impersonating ghosts, outer space aliens, gods, angels, the Holy Spirit, and God.

What Are The Voices Riplinger Hears?

If Gail Riplinger didn't hear voices nightly, then her entire ministry is a fraud. If she did hear voices—how do we know that one of them was God (she claims that the other was Satan)?

You can't avoid this issue or hide from it.

By definition, Baptists believe that the Bible is our sole authority. We don't believe that God speaks audibly to anyone today. Our only authority is the plain, clear statements of the Scripture.

Charismatics might believe such a story like Gail Riplinger's (she used to attend an Assembly of God church), but Baptists by definition, cannot.

Riplinger Practiced Transcendental Meditation

Dr. John Knapp has an interesting article on his counseling website. He describes the physical effects on someone who tries to withdraw from the practice of Transcendental Meditation.

According to Dr. Riplinger's testimony, she was a TM practitioner before she was converted.

Among the side effects mentioned by Dr. Knapp are:
"uncontrollable fatigue, sleeping during the day"
"insomnia"
"night-time hallucinations often described as visions"
"auditory and visual hallucinations"

Where have I heard this before?

He also says that TM practitioners often experience multiple divorces.

The First Question That Must Be Asked

The first question that anyone evaluating Gail Riplinger's "ministry" must answer is this—"Do I believe her claims to divine inspiration?" Is she really God's secretary? Everything depends on this. You can either believe in Sola Scriptura or you believe in something more.

Is Gail Riplinger really a modern-day Ezekiel or Deborah as she claims for herself? Is everything really for the "Greater Glory of Gail?"

What kind of megalomania does it take to compare yourself to Deborah or Ezekiel? All for the "Greater Glory of Gail."

Now you know why someone who has no training in Greek and Hebrew can consider herself the greatest living authority on Greek or Hebrew. She is just "God's secretary." The words are God's. Now you know. Gail Riplinger can offer new doctrines. According to her, the words and the doctrine come from the Holy Spirit.

Interestingly, Gail Riplinger quotes King James on the subject of extra-Biblical revelations, "Prophecies and visions are now ceased, all spirits that appear in these forms are evil." (*In Awe of Thy Word*, p. 577). Amen!

But he that doeth **truth** *cometh to the light, that his deeds may be made manifest, that they are wrought in God.*

John 3:21

CHAPTER 5
CLAIMS OF SUPERNATURAL VISITATIONS

A Common Claim

It is common for religious teachers to claim supernatural visitations and communication. No one can count all the religions and religious movements that have been started by such claims.

Baptists (who by definition believe that the Bible is the sole authority) reject all such claims of modern supernatural revelation. Baptists believe that such revelation ended with the inspiration of the Book of Revelation.

Modernist Bible translator J. B. Phillips claimed that he was visited by the "ghost" of author C. S. Lewis. In his book about Bible translation, *Ring of Truth* (p. 118-119) he claims:

> "Many of us who believe in what is technically known as the Communion of Saints must have experienced the sense of nearness, for a fairly short time, of those whom we love soon after they have died. <u>This has certainly happened to me several times.</u> But the late C. S. Lewis, whom I did not know very well and had only seen in the flesh once, but with whom I had corresponded a fair amount, gave me an unusual experience. <u>A few days after his death, while I was watching television, he 'appeared' sitting in a chair within a few feet of me</u>, and spoke a few words which were particularly relevant to the difficult circumstances through which I was passing. He was ruddier in complexion than ever, grinning all over his face and, as the old-fashioned saying

has it, positively glowing with health. The interesting thing to me was that I had not been thinking about him at all. I was neither alarmed nor surprised nor, to satisfy the Bishop of Woolwich, did I look up to see the hole in the ceiling that he might have made on arrival! He was just *there*—'large as life and twice as natural.' A week later, this time when I was in bed, reading before going to sleep, he appeared again, even more rosily radiant than before, and repeated to me the same message, which was very important to me at the time. I was a little puzzled by this, and I mentioned it to a certain saintly bishop who was then living in retirement here in Dorset. His reply was, 'My dear J—, this sort of thing is happening all the time.'"

Three Possible Explanations

to Supernatural Visitations

J. B. Phillips

Bible believers know how to respond to this claim of supernatural revelation. We do not believe that the ghost of C. S. Lewis appeared to J. B. Phillips. There are three possible explanations for his story:

1. Either a demon appeared to him and falsely claimed to be C. S. Lewis (see I John 4:1-4), or

2. Phillips was crazy as a loon, or

3. He lied about the experience. No matter which story you believe, Phillips is clearly not qualified to be a spiritual leader.

Oral Roberts

Oral Roberts claimed that a 90-foot high Jesus appeared to him and told him that he must raise several million dollars quickly or God would kill him. I do not know a single Baptist who believed him.

There are three possible explanations for his story. (1) Either a demon deceived him, or (2) he was crazy, or (3) he lied to his followers as part of a fund-raising scheme.

Mohammed

Mohammed claimed that angels appeared to him and dictated the teachings of the Koran to him. There are three possible explanations for his story. (1) Either he was misled by demons, (2) he was crazy, or (3) he was a fraud.

Charles T. Russell

Charles T. Russell claimed to "hear" the voice of God speaking to him audibly. Based on what he learned from the "voice of God," he began the Jehovah's Witness movement. Baptists don't believe his story. There are three possible explanations for his story. (1) A demon spoke to him, or (2) he was crazy, or (3) he was a fraud.

Ellen G. White et al.

Ellen G. White (Seventh Day Adventists) claimed that the Holy Spirit possessed her. Both Victor Paul Wierwille (The Way) and Moses David Berg (The Children of God) claimed to audibly hear the voice of God. Joseph Smith (Mormons) claimed that angels appeared to him. Both Aimee Semple McPherson and Kathryn Kuhlman claimed direct revelation from God.

Is There Any Difference in Riplinger's Claims?

Bible-believing Baptists know how to respond to such claims. Either a demon deceived these people, or they were crazy, or they were frauds. What is different about Gail

Riplinger's claims to divine revelation? Do you really believe she is "God's secretary?" Did God get by without a secretary for 2,000 years and then suddenly develop a need for one? Why would he pick Gail Riplinger to play a role no one has played for 2,000 years? How do you distinguish between Gail Riplinger and all the others who claim to be the agents of divine revelation?

Baptists, by definition, do not accept claims like those made by Gail Riplinger. Her entire ministry is based upon such claims!

By the way, Dr. Riplinger should not be blind to the possibility of demonic deception. Her second husband, Frank Kaleda, (the one she began with in the "ministry,") wrote a book about demonic deception called *The Shining Ones.*

CHAPTER 6
ACADEMIC QUALIFICATIONS

Impressive Academic Qualifications?

Dr. Riplinger's supporters claim that her "supernatural communications" are not the only basis for her "ministry." They point out her impressive academic qualifications.

At first glance, the "about the author" section of her books looks very impressive: college degrees, textbooks written and published, experience as a professor at Kent State University, academic awards, etc.

Many pastors promote Gail Riplinger as a well-qualified linguist and historian. They talk about her training, teaching, and experience in these areas.

One website lists her as a Harvard professor. Several websites list her as a graduate of Cornell and Harvard.

At second glance, her "resume" is very, very vague. She allows her supporters to fill in the blanks. Compare her resume to the "about the author" section of any other book. She is uniquely vague.

The Real Academic Qualifications of Riplinger

In reality, Mrs. Riplinger received a Bachelor of Arts degree in Interior Design in 1978. She received a Master of Arts degree in Home Economics in 1980 and a Master of Fine Arts degree in 1983. All of these degrees are from Kent State University.

Her six textbooks (which most pastors think dealt with linguistics and history) are as follows:

1. 1. *Restaurants:*   *A Guide for Architects,*

Designers and Developers (published originally as her M.F.A. thesis, 1983).

2. *Plants & Interiors: Guide for Environmental Designers* (publication year not specified).

3. *Design Process: A Guide for Designers & Architects* (published in 1983).

4. *Forms & Space Function: Beginning in Environmental Design* (published in 1983).

5. *Visual Merchandising & Store Design* (published in 1983).

6. *Offices: A Guide for Designers* (published in 1982).

She never explains what her "post-graduate" work at Cornell or Harvard involved but she is not a graduate of either school.

She claims that her textbooks were accepted for publication by Prentice Hall (a very large textbook publisher), but Prentice Hall never published any of them.

She mentions that she is in several editions of *Who's Who*. She forgets to mention that anyone who is willing to pay the fee can buy a listing in any of the *Who's Who* publications. She mentions an invitation to participate in President Reagan's Citizen Ambassador Program. She forgets to mention that the program was available to any academic who was willing to finance their own trip abroad.

Dr. Riplinger allows her supporters to misrepresent her qualifications. I wonder how many books she would have sold if she had honestly listed her college degrees and textbooks written. I wonder how many Baptist pulpits she would have stood behind if she had been open and transparent about her qualifications.

A Linguistics Expert?

Gail Riplinger's supporters claim that she is a linguistics expert. She describes herself that same way. In an interview with the Action 60s program, she states:

> "And, ah, so far as my background in linguistics, I taught English for three years, Ah, and in my classes, it was English for the foreign born . . .none of which spoke one word of English, and I had to teach them . . . the English language. So, of course, I became a linguistics expert after three years of doing that."

That's right, Gail Riplinger thinks that three years experience in teaching English as a second language makes her an "expert" in linguistics.

A Self-Appointed Scholar & Expert

I pastor in Chicago. There are many people here who teach English as a second language—hundreds, if not thousands. I know several. Not one of them would claim to be an expert in linguistics. To claim to be an expert with such slender qualifications is really an advanced case of megalomania.

In a November 19, 2009 interview with a Baptist radio station, Dr. Riplinger claimed to be a teacher of "history and linguistics." She may be, but she is a teacher without any qualifications.

Dr. Riplinger is a self-appointed "scholar" and a "self-proclaimed" expert.

He shall send from heaven, and save me from the reproach of him [or her] that would swallow me up. Selah. God shall send forth his mercy and his **truth**. *[Editor's addition]*

Psalms 57:3

CHAPTER 7
QUOTATIONS AND CITATIONS

Frequent Misquotes & Misrepresentations

Mrs. Riplinger's followers are fond of saying that she has proved her positions through extensive documentation and quotations.

Actually, Dr. Riplinger is sometimes capable of very good research. If an idea of hers can be supported by the facts, she will do an excellent job presenting the facts. There are chapters in her books with impressive ideas and accurate documentation.

However, when her ideas cannot be supported by the facts, she presents her ideas anyway. She blatantly misrepresents authors and the themes of their books. She routinely misquotes authors and manufactures quotes. This is very obvious and has been documented in many places.

How Riplinger Misrepresents

A favorite tactic of Dr. Riplinger is to quote someone and to offer several pages in different parts of a book as the documentation for the quotation. She pieces different statements together as if they were one statement. Of course, when she does this, she is always misrepresenting the person she is quoting. This is always improper and dishonest. She would never do this if she could use a real quote. She never allows the facts to interfere with any of her ideas.

Her books are a mixture of brilliance, research, emotional ravings, self-serving theology, and downright fraud. It takes a lot of time and research to figure out what is what in her books.

"For, let the ample and highly complex provision which Divine Wisdom hath made for the effectual conservation of that crowning master-piece of His own creative skill, THE WRITTEN WORD,—be duly considered; and surely a recoil is inevitable from the strange perversity which in these last days would shut us up within the limits of a very few documents [people] to the neglect of all the rest,—as though a revelation from Heaven had proclaimed that the **Truth** is to be found exclusively in them. [Editor's addition] [Dean John William Burgon, *Revision Revised, Article III*,1883, reprinted by the Dean Burgon Society, September, 2000, p. 338 (p. 384 in the PDF].

CHAPTER 8
THE DISTINCTIVE DOCTRINES
OF GAIL RIPLINGER

Five Distinctive Doctrines

ONE—THE VERNACULAR TRANSLATIONS WERE ALL INSPIRED ON THE DAY OF PENTECOST

Some of Dr. Riplinger's followers have suggested that it is slander to claim that she teaches this but it is clear in her books.

> "The *scriptural* viewpoint of vernacular scriptures shows them as 'Holy Ghost' inspired and concurrent with Greek scriptures, via Acts chapter 2. Paul, the one who penned much of the New Testament said, 'I speak with tongues more than ye all. . .' (I Corinthians 14:18). As penman of much of the New Testament, the reason for his gift was obvious. His statement would lead to the conclusion that Paul's epistles would have been 'inspired' in numerous languages and he, as well as others, would have had the gift to put the rest of the New Testament into all known languages of the day." (*Hazardous Materials*, p. 647).

> "Paul said, 'I thank my God, I speak with tongues more than ye all' (I Corinthians 14:18). Why did Paul use tongues 'more' than any other man? He perhaps wrote most of the books of the New Testament, using Greek, as well as penning editions in other languages as needed." (*Hazardous Materials*, p. 738).

> "*In Awe of Thy Word* proved that the English

Bible came directly from the gift of tongues which provided 'Holy Ghost' inspired words and Bibles for those who spoke Gothic, Celtic, Latin, Greek, Hebrew and the other languages." (*Hazardous Materials*, p. 738).

"The Acts 2 'Scriptures in tongues' as Wycliffe called them, were created directly by the Holy Ghost and were not man-made translations from 'the Greek.' These 'Scriptures' would have quickly been available in Latin, Coptic, Celtic, Ethiopic, Arabic, Hebrew and a myriad of other languages." (*Hazardous Materials*, p. 1095).

"Inspired vernacular Bibles, in a sense were born in Acts, chapter 2, when the Holy Ghost inspired men to speak the language of every nation under heaven. Gothic, the great, great grandfather of English was a major world language at the time of Christ and the apostles. Gothic benefitted from this gift, by which the Holy Ghost superintended over the preaching of the word in all the world (Colossians 1:5-6) and the translation of the Scriptures 'made known to all nations' Romans 16:26." (*In Awe of Thy Word*, p. 34).

Would anyone, anywhere believe that Acts 2 refers to writing complete copies of the Scripture unless Gail Riplinger told them that? Who has ever taught that before?

In Acts 2:1-4, Dr. Riplinger finds a record of inspired complete Bible manuscripts (from Genesis to Revelation) in all vernacular languages.

Read Acts 2:1-4 for yourself:

"*And when the day of Pentecost was fully come, they were all with one accord in one place. And suddenly there came a mighty wind, and it filled all the house where they were sitting. And there appeared unto them cloven tongues like as of fire, and it sat upon each of them. And they were all filled with the Holy Ghost, and began to speak with other tongues, as the Spirit gave them utterance." Acts. 2:1-4*

There is no mention of a written manuscript in any language in the passage. Yet today, anyone who doesn't believe that Acts 2 refers to written manuscripts in all the vernacular languages is called a liberal by the Riplingerites.

Do you really believe that God gave complete copies of the Bible in all vernacular languages on the Day of Pentecost? Is this really a fundamental of the faith?

TWO—THE KING JAMES BIBLE IS A DICTIONARY

According to *In Awe of Thy Word*, p. 1095, Dr. Riplinger claims that the King James Bible translators taught that the King James Bible was a dictionary. Read the Translators Preface for yourself and see if you find any such claim.

Of course, the King James Bible never claims to be a dictionary. No one would know it was a dictionary or how to use it as a dictionary unless they bought books sold by Mrs. Riplinger. Can you imagine what her bank account would be like if she could persuade everyone of this? According to Mrs. Riplinger and her followers, no one can effectively study the Bible without her books. This sounds much like the claims of Charles Taze Russell and Ellen G. White.

THREE—IT IS A SIN TO STUDY THE BIBLE IN GREEK AND HEBREW

Of course, it is true that the Bible never commands us to study the Bible in the original languages. Those who teach that it must be studied in the Greek and Hebrew are adding to the Scripture.

47

It is also true that the Bible never forbids study in the original languages. Gail Riplinger adds to the Scriptures when she attacks the study of Greek and Hebrew.

Throughout the ages there have been many great servants of the Lord who never learned Greek or Hebrew. There have also been many great servants of the Lord who profited from studying the Scriptures in Greek and Hebrew.

It is God who chose to originally give the Scriptures in Hebrew, Aramaic and Greek. He did not ask for Gail Riplinger's permission.

To take either extreme position is to say something about the Bible that it never says about itself.

FOUR—THE PRESERVATION OF SCRIPTURE IS A POWERLESS DOCTRINE

Read what the Scripture says about its own preservation. God's preservation of the Scriptures is an extension of His sovereign power.

FIVE—THE CONTINUAL RE-INSPIRATION OF THE KING JAMES BIBLE

Because Mrs. Riplinger has a weak definition of inspiration, she thinks that inspiration must take place continually. She defines inspiration as the power of the Holy Spirit rather than the giving of the very words by the Holy Spirit. She does not understand that the power of the Holy Spirit is inherently in the preserved words of God.

Anyone who doesn't believe these new doctrines of Gail Riplinger is attacked as a modernist and a heretic.

In her book *Traitors,* she questions the salvation of anyone who doesn't believe these doctrines.

Interestingly, several preachers who support Dr. Riplinger

have written books, preached sermons and published articles on the King James Bible issue. Before the last three years none of these publications contained any of these doctrines which are now considered fundamentals of the faith. Apparently, all these preachers used to be modernists themselves.

*But as for me, my prayer is unto thee, O LORD, in an acceptable time: O God, in the multitude of thy mercy hear me, in the **truth** of thy salvation.*

Psalms 69:13

CHAPTER 9
WHY IS GAIL RIPLINGER
SO POPULAR?

Two Reasons

I would suggest two reasons for the "Gail Riplinger craze!"

First, she has plugged into a real, genuine concern about the abuse of Greek and Hebrew language study. Many preachers and teachers use supposed "Greek and Hebrew expertise" to correct the English Bible. Some seem to think that this is the definition of Bible teaching.

The proper use of Greek and Hebrew is to help one understand the English Bible. Many people are deeply troubled about the misuse of Greek and Hebrew. Gail Riplinger has tapped into this genuine concern about a real problem. Greek and Hebrew can be abused and this is done so regularly.

Secondly, many people have a desire to tap into secret knowledge that makes them feel special. This fills people with pride—and it also blinds them to reality!

The Game Played Today

"I'm more King James Bible than you are!" is a favorite game today. Gail Riplinger gives you the chance to believe that you are privy to some secret knowledge that makes you more special than the people around you.

We would all do well to learn something from the legitimate concerns about the misuse of Greek and Hebrew. However, we would do well to remember that there is no special exalted position in being a follower of Gail Riplinger or any other human leader. It may all be for the "Greater Glory of Gail" for some but for true King-James-Bible believers it is all about the "Greater Glory of Jesus."

Riplinger's megalomania feeds the needs of other people for self-esteem.

CHAPTER 10
A FEMALE THEOLOGIAN

Some Deny Riplinger Acts Like a Theologian

Some of Gail Riplinger's defenders claim that she is not a female theologian, but rather a linguist and/or a historian. Really!

<u>She exegetes specific verses of Scripture</u> (that is called teaching). <u>She formulates doctrinal positions</u> (that is called teaching). She demands that the entire independent Baptist movement follow her new insights (<u>that is called usurping authority.</u>) She not only does this in writing, she does this from the pulpits of independent Baptist churches. See I Timothy 2:11-12. <u>If Gail Riplinger is not a female theologian, then there is no such thing</u>.

Her followers must stop criticizing women preachers or female theology professors. They are not doing anything that Gail Riplinger is not doing (see I Corinthians 14:34-35).

A Female Theologian, Linguist, and Historian?

Gail Riplinger appears to be the first female theologian in the history of Baptists. She is actually more than a theologian, she claims to have brand new information from God—information that no believers before her ever had. Information that no one can have without Gail Riplinger.

<u>Gail Riplinger has no qualifications as a linguist. You would assume from the statements she makes that she was an expert in Greek and Hebrew. She has been forced to admit that she does not know these languages.</u>

<u>Gail Riplinger is uneven as a historian. At times she provides some valuable information. Sometimes she presents</u>

THE MESSIANIC CLAIMS OF GAIL RIPLINGER

spurious information. Sometimes she just gets it wrong.

If Gail Riplinger were only operating as a linguist and a historian she would not get 1% of the attention that she gets now.

If a man was saying the exact same things in a fundamental Baptist Church that Gail Riplinger is saying, everyone would call him a Bible teacher.

The *Kingdom of the Cults* by Walter Martin is well known as a Bible college textbook. I have used it as a professor in four different colleges. On pages 249-250, Martin offers this warning:

> "It should be remembered that the Apostle Paul strictly enjoined the Christian Church to forbid women to usurp the authority of her male head, and leadership roles should more properly be filled by men where available to meet this need:
>
> Let the woman learn in silence with all subjection. But I suffer not a woman to teach, nor to usurp authority over the man, but to be in silence. For Adam was first formed, then Eve. And Adam was not deceived, but the woman being deceived was in the transgression (I Timothy 2:11-14).
>
> It can be clearly seen from the study of non-Christian cults, ancient and modern, that the female teaching ministry has graphically fulfilled what Paul anticipated in his day by divine revelation, and brought in its wake, as history tell us, confusion, division and strife. This is true from Johanna Southcutt to Mary Baker Eddy to Helena Blavatsky and the Fox sisters, all of whom were living proof of the validity of our Lord's declaration that 'if the blind lead the blind, both shall fall into the ditch.'" (Matthew 15:14b).

CHAPTER 11
QUEEN BEE SYNDROME

Theological Movements by Women

I have heard Gail Riplinger compared to other women who have founded their own theological movements.

May Baker Eddy

Mary Baker Eddy was also divorced twice. She also used trial lawyers and the threat of lawsuits to try to keep her followers under control. She claimed to be "God's scribe":

> "I should blush to write of *Science and Health with Key to the Scriptures* as I have, were it of human origin, and I, apart from God, its author; but as I was only a scribe echoing the harmonics of heaven in divine metaphysics, I cannot be super-modest of the Christian Science text book." [Mary Baker Eddy, *Christian Science Journal*, January, 1901.]

Apparently God needed a scribe as well as a secretary.

Ellen G. White

Ellen G. White claimed that God was giving her new information. To this day her followers debate whether this new information was given by inspiration or was given by God in some different way. (I have never understood the difference.) Mrs. White claimed to be evangelical and her books include some very good information about Christian history. Many of her early supporters were evangelical preachers—some of them Baptists.

Aimee Semple McPherson

Aimee Semple McPherson was responsible for the production and distribution of some excellent materials opposing evolution and the secularization of the American culture. She never spoke without mentioning the necessity of a personal relationship with Christ. She was able to maintain an unofficial movement for many years before it was organized into an official denomination.

Preacher McPherson could be as sweet as honey when flattering a supporting preacher. Each one was one of the most important preachers in America. She built her movement by sweet-talking preachers. But she could be as ferocious as a wild boar when anyone crossed her about anything—anything.

<u>Whenever anyone asked McPherson about her two divorces, she immediately targeted them for destruction. They were the enemies of God and they must be run out of "the church."</u> There could be no other reason why anyone could have a question.

She claimed that God told her that she had married the wrong person and that she was not married in God's eyes. This was followed by a divorce and a remarriage.

Kathryn Kuhlman

A similar story could be told about Kathryn Kuhlman. She claimed to have a gift of "a word of knowledge" as well as healing. She was a popular female preacher. <u>She claimed regular verbal, audible communication with the Holy Spirit</u>.

Dallas Billington, Baptist preacher from Akron, Ohio, challenged both her claims to healing and to verbal revelation from God.

Her ministry was scandalized by her divorce! Followers were forbidden to discuss it. If they did they were labeled as agents of Satan and traitors. She kept a trial lawyer on retainer to threaten anyone who discussed her divorce.

Interestingly, Joseph Chambers (a prominent Pentecostal preacher) has labeled the "Holy Spirit" who spoke to Kathryn Kuhlman as a demonic spirit guide.

All Four Women Suffered From QBS

All four women clearly suffered from "Queen Bee Syndrome" (QBS) They wanted to be the only female voice in an all male choir. All four saw to it that no other females rose to position of prominence in their movement. They got their self-esteem from being the only female under discussion.

Gail Riplinger is clearly the Queen Bee for some independent Baptists. She teaches doctrine in some churches where no other female would be allowed to lead in prayer. She is the only female to play a role in the current doctrinal disputes among independent Baptists. To my knowledge, she is the only female theologian ever in independent Baptist circles. I wonder, would any other females be admitted to the debate?

Should independent Baptists have a Queen Bee? Is everything for the "Greater Glory of Gail?"

Gail Riplinger's followers claim that it is unfair to compare her to "other Queen Bees" because she does not hold to all of their doctrines. But the points of comparison are clear. They all claim to be divinely chosen by God to bring new truth to mankind. They all claim divine revelation. There are many other stories of female messiahs that are very similar to the Gail Riplinger story.

Helena Petrovna Blavastsky

Helena Petrovna Blavatsky is the founder of Theosophy. She married young, deserted her husband, divorced him, and then remarried. She claimed that neither marriage was ever consummated. She claimed that her book, *Isis Unveiled* was dictated to her by several spirits. One of them claimed to be Jesus.

She is most famous for her book, *The Secret Doctrine*. Gail Riplinger calls it "the most wicked book ever written." (*Hazardous Materials*, p. 1008).

It is certainly an evil book. It influenced Hitler as well as several occult groups. Blavatsky claimed that she was ill while *The Secret Doctrine* was being written. She was in bed all day. At night, two spirits (one of whom was Jesus) would dictate articles to her. These articles eventually became the book.

Gwen Shaw

These types of stories are very common. Gwen Shaw founded the 'End-Time Handmaidens and Servants.' She began her "ministry" as the wife of an evangelical missionary. God "led" her to abandon him, and ten years later the marriage ended in divorce. She later remarried. She has united the occult, Hinduism, and the charismatic movement "under the cover" of an evangelical ministry.

Gwen Shaw claims that the voice of Jesus dictated her actions to her.

Marilyn Ferguson

Marilyn Ferguson is often considered the founder of the New Age movement. She was active in Transcendental Meditation. She claimed that several spirits revealed new information to her. One of the spirits claimed to be Jesus. She began to write and lecture about these new revelations. Along the way she divorced three husbands.

Elizabeth Clare Prophet

Elizabeth Clare Prophet founded the Church Universal and Triumphant. She claimed to reveal messages dictated to her by the "Ascended Masters." One of the Masters claimed to be Jesus. She taught the Kabbalah. Along the way she was married, divorced, remarried, widowed, remarried, and divorced.

Helen Schucman

Dr. Helen Schucman is the author of *A Course in Miracles*. She claimed that this course was dictated to here by the "voice of Jesus." Amazingly, some evangelical churches use this course. It is thoroughly New Age and occultist.

Joanna Southcott

Such stories are not new. In the late 1700s and 1800s Joanna Southcott presented herself as a female messiah in England. She claimed to receive direct messages from Christ for 22 years. At times she doubted her ministry. She sometimes wondered if the voice that she heard was really Satan, claiming to be Jesus. Two days before she died she said, "If I was deceived it must have been by some spirit, either good or evil." (*Strange Sects and Cults*, Egon Larsen, p. 20).

Lola A. Davis

Lola A. Davis was the wife of a fundamental missionary. She became a New Age teacher when several spirits began to dictate messages to her. She claimed one of the spirits was Jesus. She then divorced her preacher husband and started her own movement.

Alice Bailey

Alice Bailey was the founder of the Satanic Lucius Trust. She claimed that visions from Jesus led her to do this. While "in the ministry" she divorced two husbands.

Annie Beasant

Annie Beasant was married to an evangelical Anglican preacher. She abandoned him and eventually succeeded Madame Blavatsky as the leader of Theosophy. She received visions from several "Ascended Masters." She claimed that one of them was Jesus.

Gail Riplinger's claims about personal revelation are

certainly nothing new. Her desire to be the dominant female teacher in a movement of male preachers is by no means unique. It is fascinating how many female messiahs consider divorcing their husbands as the "will of God."

CHAPTER 12
HOW DOES SHE
GET AWAY WITH IT?

Riplinger's Unique Influence in The FBM

Several people have asked me how Gail Riplinger gets away with what she does in Baptist circles. In the history of the Fundamental Baptist Movement (FBM), no female has ever played the role that she plays.

There are several factors in understanding her influence.

Mrs. Riplinger is a master at flattering pastors on the phone. She knows how to make pastors feel like they are so very important to the "cause."

She also knows how to play the "helpless female victim." I think that she has been "cut a lot of slack" because she is a female. I do not believe that any male could have gotten away with what she has gotten away with.

She knows how to be cold-blooded, vicious and intimidating. She has threatened to sue several preachers for disagreeing with her. She seems to be totally without conscience when she is dealing with anyone who disagrees with her. Her normal tactic is to ignore what someone is actually saying, attack their motives and to quote many Scripture verses. These verses routinely apply more directly to her than the person she is criticizing.

People Are Afraid of Riplinger

It is amazing how many people are afraid of Dr. Riplinger. She knows no limits when she is attacking someone. She is really the "Queen of Slander." She has devoted followers who have no more conscience about what they say then she does. Her followers never ask for evidence proving her accusations.

The Sociopath Next Door

A Baptist pastor recommended that I read the book, *The Sociopath Next Door* by Martha Stout, if I wanted to understand Dr. Riplinger. By definition a sociopath is someone without a conscience. This book certainly describes the way that Dr. Riplinger operates.

She gets away with a lot because few people actually read all of her long books. *Hazardous Materials* runs 1,203 pages. *In Awe of Thy Word* runs 1,184 pages. I have asked several of her supporters if they have actually read these books all the way through. So far no one has said yes. Many pastors don't actually know what she is teaching.

She is bold and aggressive and it is difficult for anyone to stand in her way.

Instead of a meek and quiet spirit, she possesses a bold and loud spirit. She is the boldest, loudest woman in independent Baptist history.

CHAPTER 13
ARE YOU SURE?

Conspiracy Theories?

Anytime that anyone disagrees with Dr. Riplinger about anything, they are immediately accused of conspiring against the King James Bible and desiring to replace it with another English Bible.

Should Concern Over These Issues Be Moot?

Her disciples are adamant that no one could be genuinely concerned about issues like divorce, lawsuits, and woman preachers. But how do they know no one is really concerned about these things? They are not reacting to specific statements or actions. They are discerning motives, reading minds, and judging hearts without any information or proof.

Legal records prove that Mrs. Riplinger has been married three times and divorced twice. Her third marriage took place a few weeks after her second divorce. She has claimed that she was not divorced or remarried. After the publication of the relevant legal records she now claims that she has only been married once in God's eyes.

Of course, there are no Biblical qualifications for a female theologian because there is no such thing as a Biblical female theologian.

Christians disagree about the appropriate roles for divorced and remarried Christians.

Many of us will go a long way in supporting divorced and remarried Christians as long as they are honest and do not try to glorify their divorce. I personally would have no problem with Mrs. Riplinger's marital record if she simply acknowledged that there were unfortunate mistakes in her past and that now she is trying to faithfully serve the Lord. However, Gail Riplinger can't admit to any mistake.

What About The Consequences

Of Riplinger's Influence?

What will happen if her attitude towards divorce begins to be copied in the churches that she is promoted in? What if church members divorce a spouse of eight years and marry someone in a few weeks and then claim a special dispensation from God? How can Dr. Riplinger's followers be so sure that no one is genuinely concerned about this? Are they that good at mind reading?

Preachers who have divorced their wives after entering the ministry are already rallying around the ministry of Gail Riplinger. For some reason, she makes them feel comfortable.

How can Dr. Riplinger's defenders be so sure that none of her critics genuinely are concerned about her role exegeting the Scriptures and formulating doctrines?

The American Baptist Convention already has many female theologians teaching seminary classes and many female pastors. There was a time when no one could have believed that could happen in a Baptist church.

Will other women be allowed to teach doctrine in independent Baptist churches? If not, why not? How can the followers of Dr. Riplinger be so sure that no one is concerned about that? Are her supporters really that good at judging people's hearts?

Riplinger's Lawsuit Threats

Dr. Riplinger has threatened to sue several Baptist preachers for disagreeing with her. How do her defenders know for sure that one no one is really offended by those threats (they are clearly a violation of I Corinthians 6)? Are they that good at discerning motives? <u>What will happen if all of the church members in churches where she is promoted start following her practice.? Will they start threatening to sue their pastors every time they disagree with the pastor about anything?</u>

The Opening of "Pandora's Box"

Those who promote Dr. Riplinger are opening a "Pandora's Box."

If there is a dramatic increase in divorce among the churches that support Gail Riplinger, don't be surprised. If women start to demand theological roles in churches that support Gail Riplinger, don't be surprised. If church members start filing frivolous lawsuits against the pastors who support Gail Riplinger—those pastors will just be reaping what they have sown!

*Justice and judgment are the habitation of thy throne: mercy and **truth** shall go before thy face.*

Psalms 89:14

CHAPTER 14
IS GAIL RIPLINGER
INFALLIBLE?

Dr. DiVietro's Answer to Riplinger's Challenges

Dr. Gail Riplinger issues seven challenges (p. 1193 *Hazardous Materials*) and then dares anyone to answer them. Dr. Riplinger also calls Pastor Kirk DiVietro "one true Bible believer" (*Hazardous Materials*, p. 598). Dr. DiVietro has accepted her challenge and written the book, *Cleaning up Hazardous Materials.* He answers her seven challenges.

In her book, *Traitors*, Dr. Riplinger attacks Dr. DiVietro for daring to critique her book, *Hazardous Materials.* Apparently she did not really want her challenges answered. Apparently Dr. DiVietro is no longer "one true Bible believer." Who is he—just a mere man—just a mere pastor—to analyze one of her books?

What is Dr. Riplinger afraid of? Is she afraid that some of her theological teachings will be answered by an independent Baptist preacher? Is she afraid that some of her quotations will be examined? Is she afraid that some of her "facts" will be investigated? Since God "gave her" her books, is it blasphemous to critique what God "gave?" Maybe preachers should read *Cleaning up Hazardous Materials* for themselves and then decide.

Of course, Dr. DiVietro is now considered a conscious conspirator against the King James Bible. He must be labeled a traitor and banned from "the church" (as defined by Gail Riplinger).

Riplinger is Wrong About Dr. Maurice Robinson

One of the issues that Gail Riplinger threatened to sue Dr.

and Mrs. Waite over is Mrs. Riplinger's claim that Dr. Maurice Robinson is an editor of Berry's *Greek Interlinear New Testament*. The Waites claimed that she was in error when she made this statement and she threatened to sue them over it.

As Dr. Robinson himself has pointed out, it is impossible for him to have been an editor on Berry's *Interlinear* because it was edited before he was born. That should be conclusive.

Dr. Riplinger simply made a mistake. It happens to everyone. But Dr. Riplinger and her disciples can never acknowledge any mistake on her part. They are still adamant that Dr. Robinson edited a book that was released before his birth.

Riplinger & Her Defenders

Make Extraordinary Claims

One Riplingerite website suggests that the Illuminati planted false marriage and divorce records in Ohio courthouses to discredit her. Perhaps the Illuminati also took Dr. Robinson to the past in a time machine. We all know Dr. Riplinger can't be wrong. All for the "Greater Glory of Gail."

On page 191 of *Hazardous Materials*, Gail Riplinger claims that the inhabitants of the Kingdom of Munster (16th century Germany) are the forerunners of today's Baptists.

Actually that is a false claim used at the time to discredit Baptists. Blaming the Baptists for the fanatics in Munster is similar to blaming Christians today for the actions of terrorists like Timothy McVey.

This false charge has been answered by Baptist historians like J. M. Cramp, John Christian, Robert Torbet, H. C. Vedder, Jack Hoad, William Cathcart and Richard Cook. The Munsterites actually baptized babies and believed that they were getting new revelations from God. They were not Baptists. Of course, Dr. Riplinger's followers can't accept that. All the

Baptist historians are wrong! Gail Riplinger can't be wrong. All for the "Greater Glory of Gail"

Since Dr. Riplinger gets her information the same way that Ezekiel got his (inspiration), how could she be wrong?

You assume that you possess <u>a power of divination</u> which enables you to dispense with laborious processes of Induction; while *I,* on the contrary, insist that the **Truth** of the Text of [the original] Scripture is to be elicited exclusively from the consentient testimony of the largest number of the best COPIES, FATHERS, VERSIONS. [editor's underlining and addition] [Dean John William Burgon, *Revision Revised, Reply to Bp Ellicott,* 1883, reprinted September, 2000, p. 518, (p. 564 in the PDF)].

CHAPTER 15
THE FRUIT OF GAIL
RIPLINGER'S "MINISTRY"

The Schismatic Among Us

King James Bible believers have never been so divided. This is directly the result of Gail Riplinger's "ministry." Her followers have forgotten who the enemy is. They turn all their wrath on those who will not follow the person of Gail Riplinger. They divide King James Bible believers into smaller and smaller groups.

The door has been opened for female theologians in fundamental Baptist institutions. In some Protestant denominations, a majority of the theology teachers are women. In one prominent seminary all of the theology teachers are women. But long before a majority of theology teachers were women, there was a first female theology teacher. I'm sure a good excuse was given for breaking that barrier.

Translations Have Been Affected

Opposition has been provided for many good translation projects. Received-text Bible translators now face even more challenges and opposition from Riplingerites than they do from the Critical Text crowd.

Scripture is not just the words of men that God breathed life into, Scripture is the very breath of God. Scripture is words that God gave to man.

Bad translations are flourishing. Men do the first draft of a translation and call it "inspired." That is what Dr Riplinger has taught them to call their work. Translators then become closed to any kind of purification process like the one followed by the translators of the King James Bible or the teams led by William Carey. Shallow translators stubbornly defend their first draft on the grounds that it is "inspired."

The Doctrine of Preservation is Belittled

The Bible doctrine of preservation is belittled by the followers of Dr. Riplinger. According to Dr. Riplinger, preserved words are "museum words or accurate but lifeless equivalencies." *Hazardous Materials*, p. 1133. Where in the Bible do you find such nonsense? IN REALITY, GOD'S PRESERVED WORDS ARE FULL OF ALL THE STRENGTH AND MAJESTY OF THE SOVEREIGN GOD WHO GAVE THEM.

The Doctrine of Inspiration is Weakened

In actuality, the Riplingerites have weakened the doctrine of inspiration. They use the word inspiration often but they provide a weak definition of it. Gail Riplinger defines inspiration as "a divine influence upon human beings, as that resulting in the writing of the Scriptures." She gets this definition from *Webster's New World Dictionary* (see *Hazardous Materials*, p. 1138).

According to the King James Bible, inspiration is much more than influence. Inspiration is the giving of the Scripture. Inspiration is more than influence, guidance, or super-intendence. Inspiration is God giving the very words of Scripture (see my 1999 book, *The Means of Inspiration*).

In *New Age Bible Versions* it appeared that Mrs. Riplinger was a supporter of the Received Text. Now she and her followers are obsessed with destroying the Received Text and replacing it with new revelations from Gail Riplinger. They are obsessed with destroying the same text that Satan has spent centuries trying to destroy.

Is Inspiration an Ongoing Apostolic Gift?

Some modernists admit that the Bible is influenced by God. They don't admit that God gave the very words. Charismatics refer to inspiration but they often define it as an ongoing apostolic gift. Any definition that falls short of seeing inspiration, as God giving the very words of Scripture is a door opener for future modernism.

The Most Effective Weapon of Satan

Of course, the critics of the King James Bible try to lump every King James Bible believer in with Gail Riplinger. They try to paint all of us with the same brush. They blame all of us for her lack of integrity. They mock of all of us because of her emotional fantasies.

Gail Riplinger is currently the most effective weapon that Satan has for the undermining of the King James Bible and other good Received Text translations around the world.

*Thou art near, O LORD; and all thy commandments are **truth**.*

Psalms 119:151

CHAPTER 16
DOESN'T GAIL RIPLINGER
TEACH SOME GOOD THINGS?

The answer is yes! Ellen G. White wrote passionately about religious liberty. That does not make her a godly Christian leader.

J. K. Van Baalen popularized the statement by J. Stafford Wright, "The essence of deception is to speak 90 per cent truth and 10 percent error." This is from *Chaos of the Cults* (my Cults class textbook as a college student), p. 425.

In spite of all the good in her books, she has caused more harm than good.

But if, (as I humbly believe and confidently hope,) my conclusions are sound throughout, then may He enable men freely to recognize the **Truth**; [Dean John William Burgon, *Revision Revised, Reply to Bp Ellicott,* 1883, reprinted September, 2000, p. 520, (p. 566 in the PDF)].

CHAPTER 17
WHO ARE YOU KIDDING?

Trampling on the King James Bible

It is time for the devoted followers of Gail Riplinger to quit pretending that they care about the King James Bible. They regularly trample on the King James Bible at I Timothy 5:19; I Timothy 2:10-15; I Corinthians 6:1-8; I Corinthians 14:34-36; I Peter 3:4; Mark 10:12; and II Timothy 2:23. All for the "Greater Glory of Gail."

Apparently, there are a number of pastors who believe in the inspiration of the King James Bible but not in the authority of the King James Bible.

Riplingerites Need to Stop
Calling Themselves Baptists

It is also time for the followers of Gail Riplinger to stop calling themselves Baptists. This is the United States and you have the legal right to follow any teacher that you choose. However you have an ethical obligation to be honest in your identification.

Gail Riplinger offers her claims to new revelation from God as a new extra-Biblical authority.

By definition, Baptists believe that the Bible is the sole authority for faith and practice. Gail Riplinger introduces new doctrines never taught by anyone before her. These doctrines are not taught by any Bible in any version in any language, anywhere. Both Dr. Riplinger and her disciples treat these doctrines as fundamentals of the Christian faith. If your doctrine was invented by Gail Riplinger, you have no ethical right to call yourself a Baptist. The fact that you were once a

Baptist does not give you a right to the name, once the Bible is no longer your sole authority for faith and practice.

The followers of Gail Riplinger have "taken a hard turn to the left" and they should be honest about the basis for their faith—the "Greater Glory of Gail."

If you are a Riplingerite, you should be honest enough to say so!

The "ministry" of Gail Riplinger is a back-door attempt by Satan to undermine the authority of the King James Bible.

CHAPTER 18
SO WHO IS A RIPLINGERITE?

Who is a Riplingerite?

Let me be crystal clear. You are not a Riplingerite just because you quote Gail Riplinger. You are not a Riplingerite because you agree with Gail Riplinger about something. We all agree with Gail Riplinger about something.

You are not a Riplingerite because you have profited from some of Dr. Riplinger's research. There are sections in all of her books where she has done good research, backed with valid sources. You always have to double check her work because she has done so much faulty research in places. But, in some places she has done excellent work!

You are not a Riplingerite just because you are naïve about her real claims and teachings.

However, some people do deserve the title Riplingerite.

If you believe Mrs. Riplinger's claim about divine inspiration—you deserve to be called a Riplingerite.

If you believe doctrines invented by Gail Ripinger—you deserve to be called a Riplingerite.

If you have changed your doctrinal statement (as some Baptist organizations have done) to make it correspond to Gail Riplinger's statements—you deserve to be called a Riplingerite. The Bible is the only proper basis for a doctrinal statement.

If you attack the people that Dr. Riplinger tells you to attack,—you deserve to be called a Riplingerite.

It is amazing how some of her followers will blindly repeat

Gail Riplinger's attacks on people.

In January of 2010, Dr. Riplinger sent Dr. and Mrs. D. A. Waite a letter threatening to sue them over issues as trivial as what address a letter was sent to.

This is direct disobedience to I Corinthians 6. I publically challenged her on this abomination. She claimed that her 17 page letter was "<u>gentle and private</u>." Her drones immediately began to repeat the "gentle and private" mantra.

Have you ever received a "gentle" letter threatening to sue you? Have you ever received a gentle letter in which you were mocked, belittled and attacked on every page? Her letter is posted on the Dean Burgon Society's website.

Perhaps someone should contact her trial attorney Hugh A. Richeson, Jr. (Florin, Roebig Trial Attorneys) and ask him if a lawsuit is a private matter.

Dr. Riplinger often makes statements like this, "<u>I never defend myself publicly. God is my defense</u>." She actually made this statement in her letter threatening to sue Dr. and Mrs. Waite. Actually, she is obsessed with defending herself over every little detail. Her followers believe her every vicious attack on anyone who disagrees with her about anything.

The Internet Riplingerites

Some Riplingerites are what I call "professional internet theologians." Their entire "ministry" consists of spending hours every day attacking people on the internet. They do not have a ministry that involves dealing directly with real-life people. I try to ignore all internet theologians. Their close personal relationship with their computers warps their judgment and discernment. Of course, there are many other internet theologians besides the followers of Dr. Riplinger and they are not always easy to tell apart.

CHAPTER 19
THE COONEYITES
AND OTHER SOURCES

The False Doctrine of Re-inspiration

When I first heard about Mrs. Riplinger's claims about the constant re-inspiration of the King James Bible, I knew I had heard that somewhere before! I couldn't remember where, but I knew it wasn't from Baptist preachers.

Just check books and articles from the past written by the current Baptist preachers who promote this unbiblical theory. Even though this doctrine is now considered a fundamental of the faith, they all forgot to mention it in their previous publications.

Recently, I saw the book *Heresies Exposed* by William C. Irvine on a book shelf. It was supplemental reading in my Bible college cults class 38 years ago. I hadn't looked at it in years, but it stirred a memory. In this book there is a chapter on the Cooneyites, (p. 73-78). This cult never calls itself by this name but uses geographic names instead. They call themselves the "Church at Kent" or the "Church at San Antonio," etc.

The Cooneyites only use the King James Bible. They oppose any reference book that they do not produce. They claim that even the King James Bible is dead until it is reanimated by the Holy Spirit through the ministry of one of their teachers (they allow female teachers). For them, the King James Bible must be continually re-inspired.

My Experience With the Cooneyites

I have a little personal experience with this group. They do not have many branches in the United States but they did have a branch in Kent, Ohio. They would send out young men to infiltrate Bible colleges. The young men would lie on their applications, enter the Bible college and distribute their literature and ideas to the student body. They did this at several colleges. This group sent a young man to Landmark Baptist College while I was the administrator there. He lied to us, was accepted, and moved into the dorm.

We eventually found out what was happening. Tragically, he had influenced two students by then. When I confronted him about his lying, he told me an interesting story. He told me that he was hesitant to tell me why he did what he did because I would attribute it to a demon. I told him that he was probably right, but to tell me anyhow.

He told me that the Holy Spirit literally appeared to him and audibly spoke to him. The Holy Spirit told him to infiltrate Landmark Baptist College and to lie to us. He believed that made everything all right. He told me that the Holy Spirit continued to appear in his dorm room (never with his roommate present) and continued to guide his actions.

Now, when someone tells you a story like that, there are three possible explanations for this story. The voice of the Holy Spirit is not one of them.

The Three Possibilities

(1) Either a demon appeared to this young man, or (2) he was crazy, or (3) he was lying. That should be obvious to any Baptist. Yet, that night (it was a Wednesday) a nearby independent Baptist church allowed a student he had influenced to preach for them. They were so anti-Landmark that they were willing to allow anyone else who also was anti-Landmark to preach. It is amazing that independent Baptists have no more discernment than that.

Later that night, members of the "Church at Kent" broke into our college chapel to distribute their literature. They then left town.

I cannot directly connect Gail Riplinger to the "Church at Kent." However, I find it interesting that they both come from the same small town in Ohio. They share the same doctrine of the continual re-inspiration of the King James Bible. They both belittle the doctrine of preservation. They all claim to audibly hear the voice of God.

The Commonality of Cult Leaders

It is common for "messiahs" and cult leaders to adopt teachings from several sources. For example, Louis Farrakhan's Black Muslim theology is a combination of Jehovah's Witness theology, Islam, Kabbalahistic Gematria, and the "Moorish Science Temple."

Gail Riplinger's theology is also combined from several sources. She mixes Baptist theology with Charismatic theology to create her own theological mix. She combines Cooneyite theology, with the teachings of Peter Ruckman and John Todd (an occultist who tried to infiltrate Baptist circles). More importantly, she derives her theology presented in, *In Awe of Thy Word*, from prominent Kabbalahists. This issue is so important that a separate study is forthcoming.

He that speaketh **truth** *sheweth forth righteousness: but a false witness deceit.*

Proverbs 12:17

CHAPTER 20
WHAT IS GAIL RIPLINGER'S DOCTRINE OF SALVATION?

Supporters of Riplinger Question
The Salvation of Those Warning About Riplinger

I was astonished when I first read a statement by Gail Riplinger's pastor, Dewayne Sands, questioning the salvation of Pastor Jack Schaap. Sands wrote:

> "To be called my brother in Christ, he would have had to respond with repentance to the private letter from Sister Gail, the subsequent admonitions by other brothers, and finally the pleas from many in the aggregate body of Christ. That he has not done. Therefore, according to the Bible, I am to treat him as a heathen man (Titus 3:10-11; Matthew 18:17)."

That is the most cultic statement I have ever read in forty years of Bible study. If you don't support Dr. Riplinger, —you are not a brother in Christ. If you don't apologize for disagreeing with Mrs. Riplinger then the Bible declares that you are not saved. I was amazed to read this from an independent Baptist. Interestingly, Pastor Sand's article reads stylistically just like Gail Riplinger's writings (as do many of the emails, letters, and articles written by her supporters).

Dr. & Mrs. Waite Exposed Riplinger

In July of 2009, Dr. and Mrs. D. A. Waite publically exposed Mrs. Riplinger's lies about her marital status. They did so in a Dean Burgon Society meeting hosted in the church where I pastor. Others had exposed her before that, but Dr. and Mrs. Waite had trusted her and had defended her publicly and privately. They were shocked and felt betrayed when they became aware of the legal record.

Dr. Riplinger threatened to sue the Waites over six small details. She was not challenging their account of her divorces—she couldn't. She was dealing with issues as small as what address a letter was sent to. None of the issues was important, and in general the facts were on the side of the Waites. This was clearly an attempt to intimidate this couple (in their 80s) and to punish them for daring to tell the truth about her record.

Riplinger Challenged Over Threats of Lawsuits

I publicly challenged her threat to sue the Waites as unbiblical—see I Corinthians 6. She did not repent of her lying about the Waites or of threatening to sue them.

She responded with a book called *Traitors*. In this book, she designated a number of Baptist preachers as traitors and expelled them from "the church." She never defines what church that she is the head of and that she is expelling them from. She apparently made the decision by herself.

She claims Matthew 18 as justification. Apparently, she does not know that Matthew 18 refers to a local church setting.

Those who oppose Gail Riplinger are compared to Judas (who does that make Gail Riplinger?). Her opponents are all consigned to the same fate as Judas—an eternity in Hell.

Salvation Linked to Riplinger

In *Traitors,* salvation is based upon your relationship to Gail Riplinger. No leader of any Protestant church can claim such authority. Leaders of some cults make such a Messianic claim. The Roman Catholic pope makes such a claim about his authority. Only a Messiah can claim that those who oppose them are going to Hell. Gail Riplinger actually thinks that II Timothy 3:1-7 applies to anyone who refuses to follow her or who opposes her ungodly lifestyle.

When I first read *Traitors*, I felt sure that every Baptist would immediately see through the papal claims made by Gail Riplinger.

Since Gail Riplinger and her followers believe that salvation is based upon following Gail Riplinger, what reason is there to believe that they understand that we are saved by grace through faith. What is their gospel?

If the shed blood of Jesus Christ is the basis for our redemption, then *Traitors* is the worst form of heresy.

Does anyone know of any Baptist pastor, teacher, or evangelist who has ever claimed that they could expel someone from some world-wide church?

Does anyone know of any Baptist pastor, teacher, or evangelist who has ever claimed that those who disagree with them must not be saved?

These are truly Messianic claims. They are genuine megalomania.

"If all this does not constitute a valid reason for descending into the arena of controversy, it would in my judgment be impossible to indicate an occasion when the Christian soldier is called upon to do so:—rather because certain of these who, from their rank and station in the Church, ought to be the champions of the **Truth**, are at this time found to be among its most vigorous assailants." [editor's emphasis] [Dean John W. Burgon, *Revision Revised,* pp. xxxi-xxxii].

CHAPTER 21
A PERSONAL APOLOGY

Riplinger's Progressively Dramatic Teachings

Others saw through Dr. Riplinger's "ministry" well before I did. Her teaching becomes more dramatic with each new book, but it was there in the beginning. Her lack of integrity becomes more and more obvious with each new book and each new smear campaign. However, if you looked close enough,—the evidence was there in the beginning.

Many of Us Were Duped

It took me too long to figure out what was happening. Many of us were just happy to have another defender of the King James Bible on the scene. We were wrong. I was wrong. I have learned my lesson! As recently as March, 2009, I said from the pulpit of the church I pastor, "Gail Riplinger is a gracious Christian lady who has devoted herself to defending the King James Bible. I simply must disagree with her about a few things." I would not say anything similar today.

There is some valuable research in her books. Good men will no doubt continue to use this material and quote from her works.

However, as time goes on, more and more preachers will understand what she is all about.

David Cloud Warned Us

David Cloud warned us all about Dr. Riplinger in Vol. 11, issue 8 of *O Timothy* magazine in 1994. We should have listened. I should have listened.

I apologize for not coming to grips with this sooner.

*That I might make thee know the certainty of the words of **truth**; that thou mightest answer the words of **truth** to them that send unto thee?*

Proverbs 22:21

CHAPTER 22
LESSONS

First: We Must Recognize Claims

Of False Divine Revelation

What lessons can we learn from the Gail Riplinger story?

First of all, we must recognize claims to divine revelation for what they are—false theology. I do not know if she really heard voices or not nightly for six years. I do know that she did not hear the voice of God.

Mrs. Riplinger is too cunning and manipulative to be crazy. It is easy to believe that her claims are a complete fraud. That may be true.

Jesse Penn Lewis Warns

Jesse Penn Lewis warns that honest souls may be deceived. Her warning is profound:

> "Among such devoted believers, lying spirits have worked on their determination *literally* to obey the Scriptures, and by misuse of the letter of the written Word, have pushed them into phases of unbalanced truth, with resulting erroneous practices. Many who have suffered for their adherence to these 'Biblical commands,' firmly believe that they are martyrs suffering for Christ. The world calls these devoted ones 'cranks,' and fanatics,' yet they give evidence of highest devotion and love to the Person of the Lord, and could be delivered, if they but understood why the powers of darkness deceived them, and the way of freedom from their power.

The aftermath of the Revival in Wales, which was a true work of God, revealed numbers of 'honest souls' swept off their feet by evil supernatural powers, which they were not able to discern from the true working of God. And later still than the Welsh Revival, there have been other 'movements,' with large numbers of earnest servants of God swept into deception, through the wiles of deceiving spirits counterfeiting the workings of God; all 'honest souls,' deceived by the subtle foe, and certain to be led on into still deeper deception, notwithstanding their honesty and earnestness, if they are not awakened to 'return to soberness' and recovery out of the snare of the devil into which they have fallen (II Timothy 2:26).

FAITHFULNESS TO LIGHT NOT SUFFICIENT SAFEGUARD AGAINST DECEPTION

The children of God need to know that to be true in motive, and faithful up to light, is not sufficient safeguard against deception; and that it is not safe for them to rely upon their 'honesty of purpose' as guaranteeing protection from the enemy's wiles, instead of taking heed to the warnings of God's Word, and watching unto prayer." *War on the Saints*, p. 47-48

Maybe this explains Dr. Riplinger's ministry! Maybe not.

Second: We Must Verify

Second, we must learn to verify people's qualifications and claims. This is especially true if their teaching and ministry are based upon their personal experiences. If Baptist preachers had checked Gail Riplinger's academic credentials before they promoted her, we would not have the problem that we have today.

Third: Sensationalism Doen't Mean Its True

Third, we must remember that things are not true just because they are sensational.

Fourth: Do Our Own Thinking

Fourth, we should not let anyone else do our thinking for us. Verify for yourself.

Fifth: No One Is Always Right

Fifth, being right in one area doesn't make a person right in another area.

Sixth: Watch For False Women Teachers

Gail Riplinger is not the first false teacher to come along in independent Baptist circles. She won't be the last. We should be ready for the next one.

Seventh: Shallow Teaching Promotes Cults

J. K. Van Baalen also propularized the statement that, "The cults are the unpaid bills of the church." Shallow teaching and thinking create the atmosphere in which cults can make progress. The popularity of Gail Riplinger is a great indictment of the shallowness in independent Baptist circles. We must become more serious students of the Word of God.

*The preacher sought to find out acceptable words: and that which was written was upright, even words of **truth**.*

Ecclesiastes 12:10

CHAPTER 23
QUESTIONS THE SUPPORTERS
OF GAIL RIPLINGER
MUST ANSWER!

Questions Riplingerites Must Answer

Gail Riplinger's followers are fond of trying to bait those who refuse to follow her with trick questions. Here are some real questions that her followers must answer.

1. Do you believe that Gail Riplinger is "God's secretary?"
2. Do you believe that the Holy Spirit gives her the words of her books just like He did Ezekiel?
3. Do you believe that it is right for Gail Riplinger to exegete the Scriptures to a mixed audience from the pulpit of an independent Baptist church or an independent Baptist college or seminary classroom?
4. Do you believe that it is all right for Gail Riplinger to threaten to sue those who disagree with her?
5. Do you believe that Gail Riplinger can expel people from "the church?"
6. Do you believe that you cannot be saved if you don't support Gail Riplinger?
7. Do you believe that Gail Riplinger can forbid independent Baptist pastors from fellowshipping with other independent Baptist preachers?

Until Dr. Riplinger's supporters answer these crucial questions, none of their questions matter.

A hazy mistrust of all Scripture has been insinuated into the hearts and minds of countless millions, who in this way have been *forced* to become doubters,-yea, doubters in the **Truth** of Revelation itself. [Dean John W. Burgon, *Revision Revised*, pp. 236-237].

CONCLUSION

Are Riplinger's Challengers Plotting?

When you start to challenge Gail Riplinger in anyway, her followers immediately accuse you of being part of a plot to replace the King James Bible with a new English Bible. They discern this with their ability to read minds.

For the record's sake, I believe that the King James Bible is pure, perfect, infallible and inerrant. For 399 years it has impacted the world for Christ in a way that no other translation ever has. There is nothing in it that needs to be replaced or changed.

Robert Barnett's Statement

I identify completely with the statement by Pastor Robert Barnett (Dean Burgon Society meeting, July 2010):

> "God's truth in our 1769 Cambridge edition of the King James Bible is truth with no admixture of error for its content because the truth God revealed in His inspired, inerrant, infallible words in the Hebrew, Aramaic, and Greek was accurately translated by verbal, plenary, formal equivalence into our English language. As J. J. Ray wrote back in the 1950s—*God Wrote Only One Bible* so God's original words of truth accurately translated into any receptor language, German, French, Spanish, Russian, English etc. remains the same body of truth God originally gave by verbal, plenary inspiration in the Hebrew, Aramaic, and Greek. '. . .things equal to the same thing are equal to each other; this is the first axiom in the *Elements*.' The body of inspired, inerrant, infallible words of truth within God's Hebrew, Aramaic, and Greek words

underlying our King James Bible was accurately translated into our own English language by divine, providential preservation so as to remain without need of human correction. By that we mean it has been, is now, and shall ever remain our English Bible standard of truth. God's Truth to Me, will always be the King James Bible."

The Authority of the King James Bible

It is because of my belief in the authority of the King James Bible that I must oppose the "ministry" of Gail Riplinger.

I do not expect many of the adherents of Gail Riplinger to change no matter how much evidence they are presented with.

What Charles Surrett Says

Charles Surrett says it well:

"Regardless of what position Fundamentalists have taken on the textual issue, there is always the danger of allowing pride to dominate, hidden behind the mask of 'conviction.' Once an individual has publicly articulated his position (as in a sermon, lecture, book, or position paper), it becomes increasingly difficult to ever consider changing that position. Also, loyalties to denominations, institutions, and personalities further complicate the process of seeking the truth at all costs. This is a temptation that Fundamentalists must avoid. As Mr. Joel Spencer, one of this author's colleagues, has so succinctly stated, 'It does not matter *who* is right; it matters *what* is right.'" Charles Surrett, *Which Greek Text*, p. 112-113.

A Revealing Statement From Riplinger

I conclude with a statement from Gail Riplinger that I agree with. In fact, the statement is profound.

"Bible students are the direct target of the devil. If he can get them, when they are young and impressionable, he can have the whole church that they pastor when they graduate." (*Hazardous Materials*, p. 1,067).

Students trained in Gail Riplinger's theology are already replacing soul winning with a "ministry" of being professional critics of King James Bible believers. They are replacing the teachings of the King James Bible with doctrines invented by Gail Riplinger. What a tragedy!

Satan Must Be Laughing

Never in the history of the United States have our liberties been so threatened! We are sliding into degeneracy and socialism. Never have bold preachers of righteousness been so needed. Yet the main thrust of the ministry of Dr. Riplinger and her followers is to make war on as many King James, Bible-believing, independent Baptist pastors as possible.

Satan must be sitting back laughing!

*But speaking the **truth** in love, may grow up into him in all things, which is the head, even Christ:*

Ephesians 4:15

INDEX OF WORDS AND PHRASES

*For the hope which is laid up for you in heaven, whereof ye heard before in the word of the **truth** of the gospel;*

Colossians 1:5

ABOUT THE AUTHOR

Dr. Phil Stringer, Ph.D. is the pastor of the Ravenswood Baptist Church of Chicago. He is the former president of Landmark Baptist College. He is an active Bible Conference speaker, having spoken at over 325 churches, camps, Christian schools and colleges. He has spoken in forty-six states and eleven foreign countries. He has appeared on over 30 radio and T.V. programs. He is a visiting professor for Asia Baptist Bible Seminary (Manila, Philippines), Landmark Baptist College (Manila, Philippines), Midwestern Baptist College (Pontiac, Michigan), and Dayspring Bible College (Lake Zurich, Illinois). He serves on the Advisory Councils for Heritage Baptist College (Franklin, Indiana), Indiana Fundamental Baptist College (New Paris, Indiana), First Light Baptist Mission, the Graceway Bible Society (of Canada) and the Dean Burgon Society. He is President of the William Carey Bible Society. He is the author of several books and booklets including: *The Faithful Baptist Witness, The Transformation, Fifty Demonstrations of America's Christian Heritage, The Bible and Government, The Culture War, The Real Story of King James I, Biblical English, The Means of Inspiration, The History of the King James Bible, In Defense of 1 John 5:7, Misidentified Identity, Many Infallible Proofs, The Westcott and Hort Controversy, Verbal Preservation, Ready Answers,* and *the DaVinci Code Controversy.* He has also written several Christian school curriculums on such subjects as Baptist History, Current Events, U.S. History, U.S. Government, and U.S. Presidents. He also speaks to Civic and Conservative groups on topics related to Current Events and America's Christian Heritage. EDUCATION: 1975 Bachelor of Science in Bible, Indiana Baptist College, 1980 Master of Arts in Christian Education, Freedom University, 1997 Doctor of Philosophy in English Bible, Landmark Baptist College, 2004 Doctor of Religious Education, American Bible College. HONORARY DEGREES: 2002 Doctor of Divinity—Asia Baptist Bible College, Manila, Doctor of Literature—American Bible College.

MINISTRY EXPERIENCE: Youth Pastor, Evangelist, Bible College Professor and Administrator, Camp Director, and Pastor. ORDINATION: 1975 Lifegate Baptist Church, Indianapolis, Indiana.

LaVergne, TN USA
03 March 2011
218670LV00001B/5/P